Elizabeth M. Potter /
Beatrix Potter

Beatrix Potter
Painting Book part 4

by
Elizabeth M. Potter

Content   Page

Colouring pictures

I.	The Tale of Johnny Town-Mouse	3
II.	The Tale of Pigling Bland	11
III.	The Tale of Samuel Whiskers	19
IV.	The Tale of Little Pig Robinson	27
V.	Original book illustrations	35
VI.	Further books of Elizabeth M. Potter	40

Bibliografische Information der Deutschen Nationalbibliothek:
Die Deutsche Nationalbibliothek verzeichnet diese Publikation in der Deutschen
Nationalbibliografie; detaillierte bibliografische
Daten sind im Internet über http://dnb.dnb.de abrufbar.

© 2018 Elizabeth M. Potter 1. Auflage
Covergrafik, Texte und Bilder: © 2018 Elizabeth M. Potter

Herstellung und Verlag: BoD – Books on Demand, Norderstedt

ISBN: 9783752842296